BUILDING BLOCKS OF PARENTING

SEVEN LESSONS FROM A MOM OF SEVEN

SYBIL F. BULL

Just Appetizers: Building Blocks of Parenting

Copyright © 2024 by Sybil F. Bull

Paperback ISBN: 979-8-9921640-0-8

Printed in the United States of America

Book Design by Brand It Beautifully™ www.branditbeautifully.com

DEDICATION

To God, who taught me how to be a mom to my seven incredible children and whose guidance and love have been my unwavering foundation.

To my Grandmother, the first woman to parent me, whose wisdom and strength planted the seeds of motherhood in my heart.

To my Mom, Angela Stephenson, who loved me deeply, trained me for life and profoundly impacted the mother I became to my children.

To Aunt Hopie, Aunt Faye, and Aunt Beverly, my other moms in my younger years, who nurtured and supported me through every step of my journey.

To Mother Goldsberry and Mother Saulsbury, who became my mentors and family, offering me wisdom, love, and a guiding hand when I needed it most.

To my husband, Dwayne L. Bull, my partner in this beautiful journey of parenthood, whose love and support I could not have done this without.

To my seven children, Joshua, Jessica, Ra'chelle, Renee, Jasmine, Jeremiah, and Janesha, who are gifts from God. You have taught, loved, and helped me become a more incredible version of myself. Your presence in my life is a testament to God's grace and love.

To my grandson Sean, your presence brings boundless joy and inspiration. Your vibrant spirit reminds me daily of the beauty of life and the enduring legacy of love.

To my extended family, friends, and community, your unwavering support and love have been a beacon of hope and strength.

To all the women who encouraged me, supported me, and prayed for me, your kindness and strength have carried me through the highs and lows of motherhood.

With deepest gratitude and love,

Sybil F. Bull

Author | Wife | Coach

www.sybilbull.com

TABLE OF CONTENTS

FOREWORD

JOSHUA BULL

I have over 1100 journal entries spanning the last ten years, and my mom is mentioned in over a fifth of them. 229 times. That's a lot of mentions. I had a lot going on, most of it recovering from the consequences of my own actions. But seriously, that barely makes tangible her presence in my life. She is a fundamental reason that I'm not a sad silly man, going through life rudely using the wrong salad fork at dinner. My mom and dad are the reason I exist. Both literally, but also in the metaphysical, nature versus nature, way. Who I am, as a collection of choices, preferences, relationships and conscious being are so deeply intertwined with the deep selflessness she brought and brings to being my mother everyday.

No one was more shocked than me to find out my mother is human. That she has the same hours in the day as me, the same genes, the same imperfections as all of us. She's not perfect. Yet she found a way to love us perfectly. Unconditionally, as she'll share more about in the coming pages. And as studies have found, and as I have lived, there is nothing better than being loved well as a child.

Even the way this beautiful book is structured is on purpose. Learning first to love, by way of understanding, in order to communicate through that love and empathy is exactly how she was and is with us. And the fact that it's not all ooey-gooey, that discipline is required, learning how to hold while learning not to cling. It's all necessary. And to be clear, when I say us, I mean her and my dad's seven kids. The Syblings, we call ourselves. Being able to be ourselves, well, I'll speak for myself, having the space to be myself made me who I am. To be introverted, and curious, and almost incorrigibly obsessed with taking apart every electronic device I could get my hands on. That space to be me was amazing. Because in a lot of ways, I am, as an adult, the space they gave me as a child. Because I needed the practice as a child to realize being a little weird is actually normal. And there's no need to conform to other people's sense of cool.

I'm obviously biased but every parent or parent-to-be should read this beautiful book. The food metaphors decelerate the in your face difficulty that can come with caring for a new being. She hits on not just taking care of your child, but also taking care of yourself. In a way, it's written to be comfort food that you're actually better off for, and it works. Because just like a recipe, there is no one ingredient that makes you a healthy human, an effective partner or great parent. There are many.

But don't listen to me, dive into this recipe book for better parenting and find out for yourself.

WELCOME

Welcome to the journey of parenting, where every day presents new opportunities for growth, love, and connection. As a mother of seven, I've walked a path filled with joyous triumphs and heartfelt challenges. I've discovered that parenting is much like preparing a series of delightful appetizers—each small bite, though seemingly simple, holds the potential to nourish, delight, and sustain us through life's grandest feast.

In *"Just Appetizers: Building Blocks of Parenting - Seven Lessons from a Mom of Seven,"* I invite you to explore these bite-sized principles that can transform your approach to raising children. Each lesson is crafted to provide the essential ingredients to foster a loving, nurturing, and resilient family environment. Like the perfect appetizer, these lessons are designed to be easily digestible yet profoundly impactful, offering practical insights and heartfelt encouragement.

As parents, we are the architects of our children's futures. Our role is rewarding and challenging, requiring us to continually adapt, learn, and grow. This book is a testament to the journey I've been on – a journey filled with laughter, tears, mistakes, and triumphs. Through it all, my faith and love for my children have been my guiding lights, illuminating the path even in the darkest times.

Each chapter in this book represents a lesson learned from the heart of my bustling household. These lessons are theoretical concepts and lived experiences distilled into practical wisdom you can apply to your parenting journey. From cultivating empathy and love to mastering communication and discipline, each chapter is a stepping stone toward becoming your best parent.

THE JUST APPETIZER METAPHOR:

Think of these lessons as appetizers in the grand meal of life. Just as appetizers set the stage for a memorable dining experience, these small but powerful principles lay the foundation for a fulfilling parenting journey. They are meant to be savored, pondered, and integrated into daily interactions with your children. Like a perfectly crafted appetizer, each lesson offers flavor, nourishment, and satisfaction, preparing you for more profound, richer experiences.

In *"Just Appetizers: Building Blocks of Parenting - Seven Lessons from a Mom of Seven,"* you will find:

- **Empathy**: Learn to see the world through your child's eyes, fostering a deep connection and understanding to guide them through life's challenges.
- **Love**: Discover the transformative power of unconditional love and how to express it uniquely to each child, recognizing their needs and strengths.
- **Communication**: Master the art of effective communication, building bridges of trust and openness that will strengthen your family bonds.

- **Discipline**: Approach discipline with love and respect, setting boundaries that teach responsibility and self-regulation.
- **Independence**: Encourage your children to explore their world confidently, nurturing their independence and self-reliance.
- **Patience**: Cultivate patience as a vital tool in your parenting toolkit, allowing for growth and learning at each child's unique pace.
- **Emotional Wellness**: Prioritize your emotional wellness, understanding that a well-nourished parent is essential for a healthy, happy family.

As we embark on this journey together, I want you to know that you are not alone. Parenting is a communal experience, and we learn and grow by sharing our stories, triumphs, and struggles. This book will be a source of motivation, hope, and insight for you, offering lessons and a sense of companionship and encouragement.

So, take a deep breath and dive into these seven lessons. Let's savor each one, allowing it to nourish and inspire us as we continue on the most rewarding journey – raising humans. Together, we can build a foundation of love, understanding, and resilience to carry our children into a bright and beautiful future.

Sybil F. Bull

One

NURTURE WITH LOVE

 Love in a family is like a garden with various flowers; each child blooms differently, requiring unique care, attention, and admiration to flourish.

SYBIL F. BULL

INTRODUCTION: THE IMPORTANCE OF LOVE IN PARENTING

Love is the heartbeat of parenting. It's the foundation, the force, and the fire that lights our way as we guide our children through life's ups and downs. As a mother of seven, I have learned that while love itself is endless, its expression must be as unique as each child. Love in a family isn't just a blanket feeling that we passively experience; it's an active choice—a daily practice of seeing, accepting, and celebrating the individuality of every child.

Parenting with love is about knowing each child's heart and understanding their quirks, fears, dreams, and gifts. It's about recognizing that what comforts one may not soothe another and that each child's needs are as unique as their fingerprints. True, enduring love is shown in the little moments when we choose patience over frustration, compassion over judgment, and presence over distraction.

The beauty of parenting with love lies in this daily tailoring of our gestures, words, and presence. When we commit to loving our children with intentionality, we provide them with a foundation of security, the assurance that they are valued just as they are. Through this individualized love, we're nurturing our children's hearts and fortifying their sense of self-worth and belonging in a world that can sometimes feel overwhelming. In doing so, we send a powerful message: *You are seen, valued, and cherished.*

This commitment to love challenges us to grow and adapt with our children, to become students of each child's unique essence. With every act of love, we build a home where our children feel safe, supported, and empowered. And while we may not be able to shield them from every hurt, our love becomes the grounding force that equips them with the courage to face life's challenges with resilience.

So, as we journey through this first chapter on love, let us remember that love in parenting is not simply a feeling—it is the greatest calling we answer each day, the purest gift we give, and the most enduring legacy we leave behind. In choosing love, we become the steady hand and warm heart that guides our children toward becoming the incredible individuals they are meant to be.

THE PSYCHOLOGY OF UNCONDITIONAL LOVE

Psychologists have long established the importance of unconditional love in child development. John Bowlby's Attachment Theory shows that children need a secure base to explore the world confidently. This attachment, much like the sturdy foundation of a homemade pizza crust, supports a child's emotional growth. Alfred Adler also emphasized that children who feel valued and loved as individuals develop a healthy sense of self and a cooperative spirit. Children who receive individualized love become secure, emotionally healthy individuals capable of forming meaningful connections.

CULTIVATING LOVE IN TODAY'S WORLD

In today's fast-paced digital age, expressing and nurturing love requires intentionality. It's easy to let screens, work, and busy schedules overshadow the moments of genuine connection. Like preparing a personalized pizza, showing love means blending the ordinary with the extraordinary, infusing our daily interactions with warmth, presence, and appreciation. By taking the time to listen, laugh, and share, we create an environment where our children feel valued, not for what they achieve but for who they are.

'Let all that you do be done in love.' - 1 Corinthians 16:14. In the tapestry of family, each thread of love weaves a unique pattern, celebrating the individuality of each child while creating a picture of unity.

EXPRESSING LOVE IN DAILY ROUTINES

Expressing love doesn't require grand gestures; it's often found in the simple, consistent actions that become part of our daily lives. Like the foundational ingredients in a homemade pizza, these small acts of love provide stability and security.

- **Active Listening:** Give your child your full attention, showing you value their thoughts and feelings.
- **Physical Affection:** A hug, a pat on the back, or a gentle touch can convey warmth and love.
- **Quality Time:** Share activities your child enjoys. Your presence is a powerful expression of your love.
- **Words of Affirmation:** Regularly affirm your child's worth and accomplishments.
- **Acts of Service:** Small gestures, like helping with

homework or cooking a meal together, can be powerful expressions of love.

NURTURING WITH LOVE: PERSONALIZED PIZZA

This chapter explores the concept of nurturing children with love, using the process of making a Personalized Pizza as an illustrative guide. Each ingredient represents an essential aspect of parental love and care, offering practical insights into fostering a supportive and nurturing environment for children.

INGREDIENTS AND THEIR NURTURING ACTIONS

Mini Pizza Crusts - Foundation of Love: Just as these crusts provide the base for the pizza, start each day with a foundation of love, showing your child they are cherished and accepted.

Tomato Sauce - Unconditional Acceptance: Spread kindness and warmth in all interactions, assuring your child that they are loved for who they are.

Shredded Cheese is a binding Agent of Family Love. Sprinkle love daily, even through small gestures, to nurture a close, supportive family bond.

Assorted Toppings - Celebrating Individuality: Allow each child to select their favorite toppings, representing the importance of honoring their unique tastes, interests, and personalities.

Olive Oil - Flexibility and Adaptation: Embrace a flexible approach to parenting. Just as olive oil brings all the ingredients together, let your love adapt to meet each child's evolving needs, ensuring they feel seen and valued.

Instructions for Preparing the Personalized Pizza:

Lay the Foundation: Spread the tomato sauce evenly over each mini crust, symbolizing the warmth and security of a parent's love.

Add Cheese as the Binder: Sprinkle a layer of shredded cheese, symbolizing the binding power of love that holds the family together.

Customize with Toppings: Allow each child to choose their toppings and place them on the pizza. This step reflects the importance of honoring each child's individuality.

Bake Together: Bake until the cheese melts and the crust is golden, symbolizing the fusion of love and individuality. Share these personalized pizzas while discussing the qualities that make each family member unique.

CLOSING

Parenting with love is like creating a pizza—it requires a firm foundation, warmth, and the courage to let each child choose their flavor. Our love doesn't have to look the same for every child; it can be as unique as they are. Through our passion, we build their confidence, encourage their dreams, and create a home where they know they are cherished.

Ultimately, love is the key ingredient that transforms parenting into something extraordinary. Remember that every act of love, big or small, is a gift that nourishes our children's hearts and prepares them for life's journey. Just like a homemade pizza topped with love, these moments of connection and care leave an imprint that lasts a lifetime.

PRAYER FOR PARENTS

Heavenly Father,

Teach us to love unconditionally, just as You love us. In moments of challenge, remind us that each child is a unique reflection of Your divine creation and deserving of our acceptance and admiration. Let our love be a steadfast foundation from which they can grow and thrive.

In Jesus' name, Amen!

Two

EMPATHY – UNDERSTANDING THE HEART OF YOUR CHILD

Empathy in parenting is like sunlight to a seedling; it nurtures growth, warmth, and the blossoming of the child's true potential. - Sybil F. Bull

INTRODUCTION: THE IMPORTANCE OF EMPATHY IN PARENTING

Empathy—the ability to understand and share the feelings of another—is crucial in parenting. It's not just about recognizing emotions but diving into the world from your child's perspective, feeling what they feel, and responding with care and understanding. This emotional resonance fosters a secure attachment from which children can explore the world, develop resilience, and cultivate their sense of empathy. Psychologist Dr. John Gottman emphasized in his book, "Raising an Emotionally Intelligent Child," that recognizing and respecting your child's feelings builds emotional intelligence. This is a key predictor of future success and happiness.

PARENTING STEPS: TECHNIQUES FOR PRACTICING EMPATHY

- **Active Listening**: Dr. Daniel Siegel, in "The Whole-Brain Child," underscore the importance of connecting with your child through active listening. By attentively listening to and reflecting on what you hear, you demonstrate that their feelings are not only valid but essential.
- **Emotion Labeling**: Gottman's "Emotion Coaching" concept involves helping children understand their emotions by naming them. This not

only aids in self-regulation but also strengthens the parent-child bond.

- **Perspective-Taking:** Dr. Laura Markham, author of "Peaceful Parent, Happy Kids," advocated for putting yourself in your child's shoes. This practice not only enhances empathy but also helps in finding solutions that respect everyone's needs.
- **Modeling Empathy**: Children are keen observers. By modeling empathetic behavior in your daily interactions, you teach them to treat others with kindness, respect, and understanding.
- **Empathy in Discipline**: Siegel and Bryson argued that discipline should be an opportunity for growth and learning, not punishment. Approaching discipline with empathy helps children understand the impact of their actions and fosters internal moral reasoning.

In the tenderness of our compassion and understanding, we mirror the love of the divine. 'Finally, all of you, be like-minded, be sympathetic, love one another, be compassionate and humble.' – 1 Peter 3:8"

THE PSYCHOLOGY BEHIND EMPATHY IN PARENTING

Empathy is more than an emotional response: It's a cognitive skill that involves understanding others' emotional states. This skill is vital in parenting as it influences every interaction you have with your child. According to Dr. Siegel, the neural mechanisms behind empathy involve the mirror neuron system, which enables us to feel what others feel. When parents practice empathy, they engage in neural attunement, aligning their brain's emotional center with that of their child. This attunement builds secure attachments which are essential for a child's emotional and social development. Furthermore, empathy teaches children to be understanding of and compassionate toward others, which are invaluable skills throughout life.

By incorporating these steps and understanding the psychological foundation behind empathy, parents can foster a nurturing environment that supports their child's development into a compassionate, emotionally intelligent individual.

EMPATHY IN ACTION: THE MINIATURE VEGGIE PIZZA BITES ACTIVITY

Objective: This fun and interactive activity uses the process of making miniature veggie pizza bites to teach parents practical steps for nurturing empathy in their parenting approach. Each ingredient represents an essential aspect of empathetic interaction, providing a memorable way to incorporate these principles into everyday family life.

INGREDIENTS AND THEIR EMPATHETIC ACTIONS

Miniature Pizza Bases or Baguette Slices – Foundation of Understanding:

Just as these bases serve as the foundation for our appetizers, understanding your child's feelings and perspectives forms the foundation of empathy.

> **Action Step**: Begin conversations with your child by affirming their feelings and showing that you're there to understand, not judge.

Tomato Sauce – Spreading Compassion:

Tomato sauce covers the base evenly, just as compassion should be spread liberally in all interactions with your child.

> **Action Step**: Show compassion in everyday moments, whether your child is experiencing joy, sadness, or frustration. Use phrases like, "It sounds like you're feeling..." to clarify and demonstrate understanding.

Shredded Cheese – Warmth and Comfort:

Cheese introduces warmth and holds the pizza together, similar to the warmth and security that empathy brings to the parent-child relationship.

> **Action Step**: Offer hugs, kind words, and your presence to provide comfort in times of need, reinforcing the security of your unconditional love.

Chopped Vegetables – Diversity of Emotions:

Each vegetable adds a different flavor, representing the diverse range of emotions your child may experience.

> **Action Step**: Encourage your child to express all their feelings, acknowledging the validity of each one. Help them label their emotions to better understand themselves.

Olive Oil – Smooth Over Conflicts:

Olive oil adds flavor and ensures the pizza doesn't dry out, much like empathy can smooth over conflicts, keeping relationships healthy and resilient.

> **Action Step**: In moments of disagreement, use empathy to see your child's perspective, helping to find a mutually respectful solution.

Italian Seasoning – Spice of Individuality: Just as herbs add unique flavors, recognizing and celebrating your child's individuality adds spice to life.

> **Action Step**: Celebrate your child's unique qualities and strengths, showing appreciation for their individuality.

PRACTICAL ACTIVITY

As you prepare each miniature veggie pizza bite together, discuss the significance of each ingredient and its parallel to empathetic parenting. For example, when spreading the tomato sauce, discuss how applying compassion can positively impact your family dynamics. This activity makes the preparation process enjoyable while instilling valuable lessons in empathy that can enhance your parenting approach.

ENJOYING THE MEAL TOGETHER

As you enjoy the pizza bites, reflect on the day's interactions. Discuss moments where empathy was successfully practiced and identify where opportunities for empathy may have been missed. This reflective practice, paired with the enjoyable process of making and eating a shared meal, reinforces the importance of empathy in strengthening family bonds.

PRAYER FOR PARENTS

Heavenly Father,

Lord, grant us the gift of empathy, that we may see the world through our children's eyes. Help us listen with understanding, respond with compassion, and guide with patience. May our hearts always be open to the unspoken needs and silent pleas of our little ones.

In Jesus' name, Amen!

Three

COMMUNICATION
– THE BRIDGE TO
UNDERSTANDING

INTRODUCTION: THE IMPORTANCE OF COMMUNICATION IN PARENTING

As a mother of seven grown children, I've learned that effective communication is the lifeline of a healthy parent-child relationship. It's not just about talking or listening but understanding and connecting. Communication in parenting encompasses everything from daily check-ins to deep, heart-to-heart conversations. It's how we guide, support, and understand our children as we help them navigate life's challenges. Over the years, I've seen how clear and compassionate communication fosters trust and openness, laying a foundation for lasting relationships.

PARENTING STEPS: TECHNIQUES FOR PRACTICING EFFECTIVE COMMUNICATION

- **Open Dialogue**: Create an environment where your children feel safe to share their thoughts and feelings without fear of judgment. Encourage an open dialogue by being approachable and available.
- **Active Listening**: Listen with the intent to understand, not respond. Reflect on what you've

heard to show you're engaged and clarify any misunderstandings. This validates their feelings and thoughts.

- **Nonverbal Communication**: Remember that communication isn't just verbal. Pay attention to body language, facial expressions, and tone of voice—both your own and your children. These cues can often tell you more than words alone.
- **Conflict Resolution**: Use communication as a tool for resolving conflicts. Teach your children to respectfully express their feelings and needs as well as listen to others' perspectives—model problem-solving and negotiation skills.
- **Encourage Expression**: Foster an environment where all forms of expression are valued, whether through words, art, music, or play. Encouraging diverse forms of communication can help children find their voices.

'Let your conversation be always full of grace, seasoned with salt, so you may know how to answer everyone.' – Colossians 4:6.

THE PSYCHOLOGY BEHIND COMMUNICATION IN PARENTING

Effective communication is rooted in the principles of psychological safety and emotional intelligence. According to Dr. John Gottman, creating a climate of trust and openness allows children to express their innermost feelings without fear of reprimand or dismissal. As Gottman described it, this "Emotion Coaching" concept helps children regulate their emotions and develop empathy, both of which are essential for successful interpersonal relationships.

Furthermore, the work of Dr. Daniel Siegel on "interpersonal neurobiology" highlights the importance of a reflective dialogue in developing the child's brain. Through meaningful conversations that honor and reflect the child's feelings, parents can help their children integrate emotional experiences, leading to healthier emotional and cognitive development.

Adele Faber and Elaine Mazlish, in their book "How to Talk So Kids Will Listen & Listen So Kids Will Talk," offered practical advice on engaging with children in ways that foster mutual respect and understanding. They emphasized the importance of acknowledging children's feelings, expressing your own feelings clearly and directly, and finding mutually satisfying solutions to conflicts.

REFLECT ON YOUR PARENTING: COMMUNICATION

Reflection Exercise: The Communication Garden

Objective: This exercise is designed to cultivate a 'garden' of healthy communication within your family. It is important to recognize that, like plants, each child's communication style may need different care to thrive.

Weekly Reflection Meetings: Dedicate time each week to a family meeting where everyone can share their thoughts, feelings, and experiences from the week. Use this opportunity to practice active listening and validate each other's experiences.

Communication Journal: Keep a family communication journal where family members can write down thoughts or feelings they may find difficult to express verbally. Review the journal together during your weekly meetings to address any issues or celebrate successes.

Role-Playing: Engage in role-playing exercises to practice difficult conversations or conflict resolution, helping children develop empathy and understanding from different or varying perspectives.

BITE-SIZED APPETIZER PRINCIPLE: THE COMMUNICATION CANAPÉS

Recipe Objective: These canapés represent how we communicate in our family. Each ingredient symbolizes a component of effective communication; together, they create a delightful mix of flavors that cater to different tastes, just as we cater to different communication styles.

INGREDIENTS

- Small toasts or crackers (the base, representing an open dialogue)
- Cream cheese or hummus (spreading understanding)
- Sliced vegetables or meats (diversity of expression)
- Herbs or spices (adding flavor to our conversations)

INSTRUCTIONS

Prepare the Base: Place your choice of small toasts or crackers on a serving tray.

Spread Understanding: Apply a layer of cream cheese or hummus to each base.

Diversity of Expression: Arrange sliced vegetables or meats on the spread. This layer represents the importance of encouraging diverse forms of expression within your family.

Season: Sprinkle herbs or spices over the canapés. As these add flavor, so too do respectful and loving communication enrich our relationships.

PRACTICAL ACTION STEP WITH EACH INGREDIENT

- **Small Toasts or Crackers (Open Dialogue):** Like these bases form the foundation, it's vital to establish open lines of communication with your children. Please encourage them to openly share their thoughts and feelings, ensuring they know they're heard and valued.
- **Cream Cheese or Hummus (Understanding):** The spread signifies understanding and empathy in communication. Practice active listening and empathy by reflecting on what your children say and how they feel, validating their experiences.
- **Sliced Vegetables or Meats (Diverse Expression):** These toppings represent the variety of ways your children might express themselves. Support and validate their unique methods of expression, whether through words, art, music, or other outlets, be they creative or otherwise.
- **Herbs or Spices (Flavorful Conversations):** Just as herbs and spices add depth, encourage conversations that delve deeper into thoughts and feelings. Use open-ended questions to explore your child's perspective and foster a richer dialogue.

ENJOYING THE MEAL TOGETHER

As you enjoy these communications canapés with your family, reflect on how you communicate and how you can continue fostering an open and understanding dialogue. Discuss how the variety of toppings on the canapés, like the diversity in your family, makes the experience more prosperous and enjoyable.

This activity provides a practical demonstration of effective communication principles and a delicious way to bring the family together. It reinforces the message that you can build stronger, more loving relationships through understanding and respect for each other's unique forms of expression.

THE PSYCHOLOGY BEHIND IT

Drawing upon the principles shared by Gottman, Siegel, Faber, and Mazlish, this chapter emphasizes the critical role of communication in developing emotional intelligence and secure attachments. Their research and strategies provide a solid foundation for parents striving to create a family environment where every member feels understood, valued, and connected.

By weaving these psychological insights into the daily fabric of family life, parents can guide their children toward becoming effective communicators. That means they can express themselves clearly, listen deeply, and navigate relationships with empathy and respect.

PRAYER FOR PARENTS

Heavenly Father,

Bless us with the art of communication, that our words may be bridges of connection rather than walls of division. Help us speak with kindness, listen with intention, and understand with depth, that our families may be sanctuaries of trust and understanding.

In Jesus' name, Amen!

Four

DISCIPLINE – GUIDING WITH LOVE AND RESPECT

 Discipline in our family is like gardening; we nurture, guide, and carefully tend to each unique child, always aiming to help them bloom into their best self.

SYBIL F. BULL

INTRODUCTION: THE IMPORTANCE OF DISCIPLINE IN PARENTING

Discipline, as I've understood through the bustling journey of raising seven children, is far more about guidance than punishment. It's about teaching and nurturing, setting boundaries that keep our children safe, and guiding them toward wise choices. With each child presenting unique challenges and lessons, the journey of discipline has been one of growth—not just for my children, but profoundly for myself. The essence of effective discipline lies in love, respect, and understanding. These qualities foster a child's ability to self-regulate and respect others.

PARENTING STEPS: TECHNIQUES FOR PRACTICING EFFECTIVE DISCIPLINE

Consistent Boundaries: Establish clear and consistent rules and consequences. Consistency helps children understand expectations, and the stability of these boundaries provides a sense of security.

Positive Reinforcement: Focus on rewarding good behavior more than punishing bad behavior. Recognizing and praising positive actions encourages children to repeat those behaviors.

Empathetic Listening: Before addressing the behavior, take a moment to listen to your child's feelings and perspective. Understanding the root cause of a behavior can lead to more practical guidance.

Teach Problem Solving: Use disciplinary moments as opportunities to teach problem-solving skills. Help children understand the consequences of their actions and encourage them to think of a variety of solutions.

Model Respectful Behavior: Children learn from what they see. Model the respect, calmness, and patience you wish to see in them. Your behavior teaches them how to handle their own emotions and interactions with others.

'Discipline your children, and they will give you peace; they will bring you the delights you desire.' – Proverbs 29:17.

In our journey of discipline, we seek not to control but to guide our children with wisdom and love, planting seeds of character that will grow throughout their lives.

THE PSYCHOLOGY BEHIND DISCIPLINE IN PARENTING

Effective discipline is grounded in authoritative parenting, with high responsiveness and demands. Psychologist Diana Baumrind's research on parenting styles highlighted authoritative parenting as optimal for a child's development. This approach combines clear expectations with support and recognition of the child's autonomy. Ultimately, it fosters self-discipline, responsibility, and long-lasting respect between parent and child.

Dr. Dan Siegel's work on "No-Drama Discipline" emphasized the importance of connecting with your child before correcting them. This connection-based approach aligns with the brain's development, encouraging cooperation and improving the child's ability to regulate emotions and behaviors.

REFLECT ON YOUR PARENTING: DISCIPLINE

Reflection Exercise: The Discipline Diary

Objective: This exercise encourages parents to reflect on their disciplinary approaches, focusing on moments of growth, understanding, and connection.

Weekly Reflections: After a week of implementing disciplinary actions, write down instances where discipline was required. Note what was and was not effective, as well as how you and your child felt during those moments.

Identify Patterns: Look for behavior patterns (your own and your child's) that might indicate underlying needs or triggers. Understanding these can help tailor your disciplinary approach more effectively.

Plan for Growth: Set goals for improving your discipline strategies based on your reflections. Consider areas where you can be more consistent, empathetic, or better at teaching problem-solving skills.

BITE-SIZED APPETIZER PRINCIPLE: THE HARMONY HUMMUS DIP

Recipe Objective: This hummus dip represents the blend of ingredients (discipline strategies) that create a balanced, nurturing environment in which your children may grow.

INGREDIENTS

- Chickpeas (the foundation, representing consistent boundaries)
- Tahini (blending respect into discipline)
- Olive oil (smooth communication)
- Lemon juice (adding zest with positive reinforcement)
- Garlic, salt, and spices (the variety of disciplinary approaches)

INSTRUCTIONS

Blend: Combine all ingredients in a food processor until smooth. Each component contributes to the overall flavor, just as different disciplinary approaches contribute to effective parenting.

Serve with Love: Present the hummus with an assortment of veggies and pita bread for dipping. This act of sharing mirrors how discipline, when done with love and respect, is shared within the family to nurture growth.

PRACTICAL ACTION STEP WITH EACH INGREDIENT

- **Chickpeas (Consistent Boundaries)**: As chickpeas form the hummus base, so too do consistent boundaries form the foundation of effective discipline. Reflect on your family's rules and how consistently you apply them.
- **Tahini (Respect)**: The smoothness of the tahini reminds us to blend respect into every disciplinary action.
- **Olive Oil (Smooth Communication)**: Like olive oil makes the hummus creamy, smooth

communication ensures that your children receive your disciplinary messages well. Practice clear, calm, and positive communication, especially in challenging moments.

- **Lemon Juice (Zest with Positive Reinforcement)**: Just as lemon juice adds zest to the hummus, positive reinforcement adds vitality to your discipline strategy. Focus on acknowledging and celebrating your child's good choices and behaviors to encourage more of the same.
- **Garlic, Salt, and Spices (Variety of Disciplinary Approaches)**: These ingredients add depth and complexity to the hummus, much like various disciplinary approaches can enrich your parenting. Adapt your strategies to fit the situation and your child's needs, mixing firmness with gentleness and severe discussions with playful interactions.

ENJOY TOGETHER

As you share this harmony hummus dip, use the opportunity to hold open discussions about family rules, expectations, and the importance of understanding and respecting each other's perspectives. This shared meal can become a symbolic moment of family unity and mutual respect, reflecting the balanced and nurturing environment you strive to create through your discipline practices and choices.

PRAYER FOR PARENTS

Heavenly Father,

Provide us with the wisdom to discipline with love and respect, guiding our children toward righteousness and integrity. In our teaching, let us mirror Your gentle hand and combine firmness with grace, that our children may learn the value of boundaries and the power of forgiveness.

In Jesus' name, Amen!

Five

THE BLEND OF INDEPENDENCE – FOSTERING SELF-RELIANCE AND CONFIDENCE

 In our family, fostering independence is like cultivating a garden: We provide the soil, sun, and water, but the flowers grow, reaching for the sky on their own.

SYBIL F. BULL

INTRODUCTION: THE IMPORTANCE OF INDEPENDENCE IN PARENTING

As a mother to seven unique individuals, one of the greatest gifts I've aimed to bestow upon each of them is independence. This journey has taught me that fostering independence isn't about pushing my children away but guiding them to find their own paths, make their own choices, and learn from their own experiences. It's a delicate blend of support and freedom, allowing each child to develop self-reliance and confidence as they navigate the world on their own terms.

PARENTING STEPS: TECHNIQUES FOR PRACTICING EFFECTIVE INDEPENDENCE

Encourage Exploration: Allow your children to explore their interests and passions. Through books, hobbies, or outdoor adventures, exploration is vital to developing a sense of self.

Responsibility Assignments: Assign age-appropriate chores and tasks, increasing in complexity as they increase in competence. This teaches valuable life skills and instills a sense of responsibility and achievement.

Decision-Making Opportunities: Allow your children to make choices, from selecting their clothes to managing a small budget. Guided decision-making fosters critical thinking and personal preference.

Problem-Solving Together: When challenges arise, resist the urge to solve them immediately. Instead, guide your children through finding their own solutions, encouraging creativity, resilience, and critical thinking.

Celebrate Independence: Recognize and celebrate milestones of independence, no matter how small. This reinforcement builds confidence and self-reliance.

'Train up a child in the way he should go, and when he is old he will not depart from it.' – Proverbs 22:6

As we nurture our children's independence, we equip them with a foundation of values and faith, trusting that they will walk confidently in their own paths, grounded in truth and love.

THE PSYCHOLOGY BEHIND INDEPENDENCE IN PARENTING

Promoting independence in children is deeply rooted in psychological theories of development. Psychologist Erik Erikson's stages of psychosocial development, particularly the stages of autonomy vs. shame and doubt and industry vs. inferiority, highlight the importance of fostering a sense of competence and independence in children. These stages suggest that successfully navigating such challenges leads to developing a strong sense of self and confidence.

Dr. Maria Montessori's educational philosophy also emphasizes the importance of independence in learning and development. She believed that children learn best in environments that support their natural desire to do things for themselves, encouraging exploration and self-directed learning.

REFLECT ON YOUR PARENTING: INDEPENDENCE

Reflection Exercise: The Independence Inventory

Objective: This exercise encourages parents to assess how they support their children's growth in independence.

Weekly Independence Observations: Keep a journal of moments when your child displays independence, how you supported or could have better supported these moments, and any obstacles you both faced.

Set Independence Goals: Based on your observations, set specific goals for each child to achieve further independence. These goals should be tailored to their age, interests, and abilities.

Family Independence Meeting: Hold a family meeting to discuss these goals, encourage input from your children on how they'd like to achieve them, and plan the steps together.

BITE-SIZED APPETIZER PRINCIPLE: THE FRUIT AND CHEESE PLATTER

Recipe Objective: This fruit and cheese platter represents how independence can be nurtured within the family. Each fruit and cheese variety symbolizes each child's unique path.

INGREDIENTS

- A variety of cheeses (representing different strengths and qualities)

- An assortment of fruits (symbolizing the diversity of interests and passions)
- Crackers or bread (the support system that holds everything together)

INSTRUCTIONS

Arrange with Care: Place the cheeses and fruits on a platter, inviting your children to help. Arranging their platter can mirror how you support their paths to independence, offering choices and guidance without taking control.

Serve with Guidance: As you serve the platter, discuss the unique qualities of each cheese and fruit, drawing parallels to each child's strengths and interests. Note how these can be nurtured toward independence.

Enjoy Together: Sharing this platter as a family reinforces the idea that, while independence is about individual paths, it's also about coming together to support and celebrate each other's journeys.

PRACTICAL ACTION STEP WITH EACH INGREDIENT

- **Cheeses (Different Strengths and Qualities)**: Discuss with your children how their strengths and qualities are like the different cheeses, each with its unique flavor and value.
- **Fruits (Diversity of Interests)**: Use a variety of fruits to highlight your family's diversity of interests and passions. Encourage your children to explore and embrace their unique preferences, just as they might choose different fruits from the platter.
- **Crackers or Bread (Support System)**: Crackers or bread are the foundation of the platter, much like

the support system you provide for your children. It holds everything together, symbolizing the stable base from which they can confidently explore their independence.

ENJOYING THE MEAL TOGETHER

As you and your family enjoy the fruit and cheese pattern, use this time to hold meaningful conversations about independence. Discuss the importance of trying new things, making decisions, and learning from successes and mistakes. This shared experience can reinforce the message that, while each family member is on their unique journey toward independence, the family provides a supportive and loving base from which to grow.

This chapter aims to impart the notion that fostering independence in children is a nuanced, loving process that encourages exploration, supports decision-making, and celebrates individuality. By integrating these principles into daily family life, parents can help their children develop the self-reliance and confidence they need to navigate the world on their own terms, knowing they have a robust support system to back them up.

PRAYER FOR PARENTS

Heavenly Father,

Inspire us to nurture independence in our children, empowering them to explore, make decisions, and face challenges with courage. As we support their journeys on the path to self-reliance, keep us mindful of Your ever-present guidance in our lives and theirs.

In Jesus' name, Amen!

Six

PATIENCE – WEAVING CALM INTO THE CULTURAL FABRIC OF FAMILY LIFE

INTRODUCTION: THE IMPORTANCE OF PATIENCE IN PARENTING

Patience has been my guiding thread in the grand tapestry of raising seven distinct personalities. It's a virtue that transcends mere waiting: It's an active engagement with time, growth, and the inevitable challenges of parenting. In our fast-paced world, where instant gratification is often the norm, teaching patience becomes not only a personal endeavor but a cultural imperative. It's about slowing down, appreciating the now, and understanding that some of life's most valuable lessons and experiences unfold over time. I've learned that patience allows us to see the individual needs of our children against the backdrop of societal expectations, guiding them with love and understanding through their unique journeys.

PARENTING STEPS: TECHNIQUES FOR PRACTICING EFFECTIVE PATIENCE

Embrace Cultural Diversity: Recognize and celebrate how your family's culture (or cultures) views and practices patience. Integrating these practices into daily life can enrich your children's understanding and appreciation of patience.

Mindful Pauses: Cultivate the habit of pausing before reacting. This moment of mindfulness allows you to approach situations with clarity and purpose, embodying the sense of calm that you wish to instill in your children.

Set Realistic Expectations: Understand the developmental stages of your children and set expectations accordingly. This understanding can mitigate frustrations for you and your children, fostering a more patient family environment.

Encourage Delayed Gratification: Teach the value of waiting for a reward through games and activities. This practice helps children learn self-control and understand the satisfaction that comes from anticipation.

Model Patience: Demonstrate patience in your actions and words. Children are keen observers: Seeing patience in action teaches them its value and applicability in everyday life.

'Be completely humble and gentle; be patient, bearing with one another in love.' – Ephesians 4:2.

Our family's practice of patience is a reflection of our faith, a testament to the belief that every moment of waiting is filled with the potential for growth and understanding.

THE PSYCHOLOGY BEHIND PATIENCE IN PARENTING

Patience is fundamentally about emotional regulation and managing one's impulses and reactions. Psychological research, including studies on self-control and delayed gratification (most famously, the Marshmallow Test by Walter Mischel), highlights patience as a critical component of success, happiness, and emotional well-being. Culturally, patience is a virtue that varies in expression but universally signifies wisdom, resilience, and strength.

In the context of parenting, Dr. Laura Markham pointed out that patience is crucial to forming secure attachments and fostering an environment where children feel safe to explore, make mistakes, and learn. Moreover, patience is intertwined with the concept of "authoritative parenting," a style identified by Diana Baumrind as both responsive and demanding. Research has shown that this approach can lead to positive developmental outcomes for children.

REFLECT ON YOUR PARENTING: PATIENCE

Reflection Exercise: The Patience Tapestry

Objective: This exercise invites you to reflect on how patience is woven through your family's daily life, including cultural influences and personal growth.

Daily Cultural Reflections: Note how your family's cultural views on patience have influenced your parenting. How did you integrate these practices into your approach?

Patience Challenges: Identify moments where patience was particularly challenging. Reflect on the triggers and explore strategies for maintaining calm in similar future situations.

Patience Goals: Set personal and family goals for cultivating patience. Consider incorporating cultural rituals or practices that emphasize patience and resilience.

BITE-SIZED APPETIZER PRINCIPLE: THE BRUSCHETTA OF PATIENCE

Recipe Objective: This bruschetta symbolizes the layered approach to cultivating patience within the family. Each ingredient represents a different facet of patience, from cultural understanding to the sweetness of delayed gratification.

INGREDIENTS

- Baguette slices (the foundation, representing the solid base of cultural and personal values)
- Tomato mixture (the heart, embodying love, understanding, and the richness of cultural diversity)
- Basil (freshness, symbolizing growth and renewal)
- Olive oil (smoothness, representing the ease that comes with practiced patience)
- Balsamic glaze (depth, reflecting the complex and rewarding nature of patient parenting)

INSTRUCTIONS

Prepare With Intention: Toast the baguette slices and mix the tomatoes with basil and olive oil, being mindful of each step's cultural significance and associated personal values.

Assemble With Thoughtfulness: Spoon the mixture onto each slice, drizzling with balsamic glaze as a reminder of the beauty and depth that patience adds to our lives. Each layer speaks to the careful cultivation of patience, from the foundation to the nuanced finish that completes the experience.

Serve With Reflection: Present this bruschetta to your family as a symbol of the patience woven through your collective journey. Use this time to discuss the importance of patience in achieving personal goals, understanding cultural heritage, and strengthening family bonds.

Enjoy Together: As you share this appetizer, reflect on the day's moments that tested or triumphed over your patience. Discuss how patience has influenced your family's dynamics and the understanding of your cultural background, as well as that way in which it has facilitated personal growth and resilience.

PRACTICAL ACTION STEP WITH EACH INGREDIENT

- **Baguette Slices (Cultural and Personal Values)**: Reflect on how your family's cultural background and personal values influence your understanding and practice of patience. Discuss these foundations with your children, teaching them the importance of patience in both your heritage and personal belief systems.
- **Tomato Mixture (Love and Understanding)**: Use the heartiness of the tomato mixture to talk about the role of love and understanding in practicing patience. Share stories from your culture or family history which highlight patience as a virtue.
- **Basil (Growth and Renewal)**: The freshness of the basil can lead to conversations about growth and the opportunity for renewal that patience provides. Discuss how patience has led to personal development or a more profound understanding within the family.
- **Olive Oil (Ease in Patience)**: The smoothness of olive oil represents the ease that comes with practiced patience. Share anecdotes where patience was able to transform a potentially tricky situation into a learning experience.
- **Balsamic Glaze (Complex Rewards)**: The depth of the balsamic glaze mirrors the complex and rewarding nature of patient interactions. Highlight moments where patience led to unexpected joy, learning, or deepened relationships within the family.

This chapter on patience—infused with cultural insights, psychological foundations, and practical reflections—is designed to deepen your family's appreciation for this essential virtue. By understanding patience as a multifaceted practice enriched by cultural heritage and personal growth, families can navigate the complexities of life with grace and resilience. The bruschetta of patience is an appetizer that acts as a metaphor for the layered, rich experiences that patience cultivates in the family garden.

PRAYER FOR PARENTS

Heavenly Father,

Bestow upon us the virtue of patience, that we may embody calmness and perseverance in the face of parenting's trials. In moments of frustration, remind us of the slow and beautiful unfolding of Your plan. Teach us to await Your timing with hopeful hearts.

In Jesus' name, Amen!

Seven

EMBRACING EMOTIONAL WELLNESS – A HEARTFELT JOURNEY

A PERSONAL INTRODUCTION

In the unfolding story of our lives as parents, the chapter on emotional wellness is perhaps the most transformative. As a mother who has navigated the diverse personalities and needs of seven children, I've come to understand that emotional wellness isn't just a part of the journey but its core essence. Emotional wellness, rooted in self-love and healing, is the beacon that guides us toward being the best versions of ourselves. It's from this wellspring of wellness that we can draw and then pour into our children's lives, nurturing them with love, understanding, and presence.

UNDERSTANDING EMOTIONAL WELLNESS

Emotional wellness is the ability to successfully handle life's stresses and adapt to change throughout difficult times. It's about recognizing our feelings, understanding why we feel that way, managing our reactions, and processing our emotions in a healthy manner. It's not the absence of stress or emotions but the ability to live with them, understand them, and harness them as guides rather than obstacles.

For us as parents, emotional wellness doesn't mean we're always calm or that we have all the answers. It means we're aware of our emotional states and we strive to approach both our children and ourselves with empathy and understanding. It's about being present, not perfect.

THE PATH TO SELF-AWARENESS

At the heart of emotional wellness lies self-awareness. This profound understanding of our own emotions, triggers, strengths, and weaknesses illuminates our interactions with our children. It influences how we communicate, discipline, and express love. Self-awareness allows us to recognize when our past experiences or trauma may be coloring our reactions to our children, therefore enabling us to respond from a place of healing rather than hurt.

EMOTIONAL WELLNESS IN ACTION

When we are emotionally well, our parenting reflects patience, empathy, and openness. We're able to listen actively, communicate effectively, and offer our children the understanding and support they need to thrive. It looks like taking a deep breath before responding to a tantrum, offering a hug instead of a harsh word, or simply being present in the moment with our child.

Conversely, when we are struggling emotionally, our parenting may reflect our internal chaos. We might find ourselves reacting impulsively, withdrawing, or being inconsistent with our affection and rules. It's the moments when stress overwhelms us and we snap at a question that deserved a thoughtful answer.

A MOTHER'S GUIDANCE

Emotional wellness doesn't happen overnight. It's a journey that requires commitment, patience, and grace—grace that we must extend to ourselves as well as our children. Here are a few steps to guide you on this path:

Daily Reflection: Start or end each day by reflecting on your emotions. What triggered them? How did you respond? This practice grows self-awareness and emotional intelligence.

Seek Healing: If past trauma is affecting your parenting, seek help. Therapy, support groups, and spiritual guidance are valuable resources.

Cultivate Patience: Practice mindfulness or meditation to cultivate patience and presence, allowing you to respond more thoughtfully in stressful moments.

Foster Connections: Build a supportive community around your family. Share your journey with other parents and learn from their experiences.

Embrace Your Faith: For those of us grounded in faith, prayer and scriptural meditation offer strength and perspective. They remind us that we are not alone in our struggles.

YOUR EMOTIONAL WELLNESS PLATTER

Consider creating a symbolic 'Emotional Wellness Platter' for yourself. Fill it with things that nourish your soul and remind you of your journey toward emotional wellness. It could include inspirational quotes, a list of gratitude, reminders of your strengths, or affirmations of your progress.

IN CLOSING

Dear fellow parent,

Remember that emotional wellness is a gift you give not only to yourself but also your children and everyone around you. It's the foundation upon which loving, understanding, and resilient families are built. As you navigate your journey, know that every step toward emotional wellness is a step toward a fuller, richer life for you and your loved ones.

In this journey, let's be gentle with ourselves. Embrace the process of growing, healing, and loving with open hearts and open arms. Together, we can create a legacy of emotional wellness that will enrich our families for generations to come.

PRAYER FOR PARENTS

Heavenly Father,

Heal us, Lord, from our past hurts and guide us toward emotional wellness. Strengthen us from within, that we may parent from a place of wholeness and peace. Help us recognize our worth in Your eyes. Nurture our spirits with self-care and love, that we may pour out Your love into our children from a cup that overflows.

In Jesus' name, Amen!

Eight

CRAFTING AFFIRMATIONS: THE POWER OF SPOKEN WORDS

In the closing pages of our shared journey through the art and heart of parenting, I invite you to engage in a transformative practice: the crafting of affirmations. This *Just Appetizers* principle activity is a gift you give to yourself and your children, acting as a daily reminder of the power held in the words we speak over our lives and the lives of those we cherish most.

THE PSYCHOLOGY AND FAITH BEHIND AFFIRMATIONS

Words have the profound ability to shape our reality, influence our mindset, and alter our emotional state. Psychologically, affirmations can rewire our brains, reinforcing positive thinking patterns while diminishing the power of negative self-talk. From a perspective of faith, spoken words are a testament to our belief in the unseen, acting as a declaration of our hope, trust, and conviction in God's promises.

FOR PARENTS: CRAFTING YOUR AFFIRMATIONS

When creating affirmations, consider using the acronym LOVE:

- **Light**: Affirmations should bring light into areas of darkness, illuminating your strengths and potential.
- **Optimistic**: Keep your words positive, focusing on what you wish to attract or become.
- **Verbalize**: Speak your affirmations aloud, giving voice to your intentions and beliefs.
- **Empower**: Choose words that empower and uplift you, reinforcing your ability to overcome and thrive.

Examples for Parents

L – "I am a beacon of patience and understanding, illuminating the path for my children."

O – "Optimism guides my thoughts and actions, transforming challenges into opportunities for growth."

V – "I verbalize love and encouragement, creating an atmosphere of warmth and acceptance in my home."

E – "Every day, I am empowered to make choices that nurture my family's well-being and my own."

FOR CHILDREN: SPEAKING LIFE OVER YOUR CHILDREN

Just as you nourish your spirit with affirmations, so too can you speak life into your children's hearts. Use the acronym GIFT to create affirmations for them:

- **Grace**: Words that extend grace, acknowledging their efforts and growth.
- **Inspiration**: Affirmations that inspire them to dream, explore, and discover.
- **Faith**: Declarations that instill faith in themselves and their unique journey.
- **Truth**: Speak truths that affirm their value(s), purpose, and sense of belonging.

Examples for Children

G—"You are graced with the ability to learn from every experience, growing stronger and wiser each day."

I – "In you, I see infinite potential waiting to unfold, inspiring you to reach for your dreams."

F – "Faith in yourself and your abilities lights your path, guiding you to your purpose."

T – "The truth of your worth is unshakeable; you are loved, valued, and destined for greatness."

CREATING YOUR OWN AFFIRMATIONS

Now, I encourage you to craft your own affirmations, drawing from the depths of your heart and the heights of your hopes. Let these spoken words be seeds which are planted in the fertile soil of your own and your children's spirits. Watered daily with faith and positivity, they are destined to bloom into a beautiful reality.

Remember, the journey of parenting is not just about guiding our children but also growing alongside them. As you speak these affirmations over your lives, may you witness the transformative power of love, belief, and words made manifest. This is your Just Appetizer Principle activity, which is a simple-yet-profound practice that nourishes the soul and shapes the future—one affirmation at a time.

PRAYER FOR PARENTS: A JOURNEY THROUGH THE HEART

Heavenly Father,

In the sacred journey of parenthood, we turn to You, seeking Your wisdom, strength, and guidance. As we navigate the complexities of raising our children, we ask for Your light to illuminate our paths, Your grace to fill our hearts, and Your peace to calm our spirits.

In every step of this parenting journey, may we feel Your presence, draw from Your strength, and reflect Your love. Guide us to raise our children to know You, love You, and serve You.

In Jesus' name, Amen!

REFERENCES

Gottman, Dr. John, (1997) *Raising an Emotionally Intelligent Child: The Heart of Parenting,* Simon & Schuster

Siegel, Dr. Daniel, (2011), *The Whole-Brain Child: 12 Revolutionary Strategies to Nurture Your Child's Developing Mind,* Delacorte Press

Markham, Dr. Laura, (2012), *Peaceful Parent, Happy Kids: How to Stop Yelling and Start Connecting,* Perigee Books

Campbell, Dr. Ross, (1977), *How to Really Love Your Child,* David C. Cook

Chapman, Gary (1997), *The 5 Love Languages of Children: The Secret to Loving Children Effectively,* Northfield Publishing

Newman, Ph.D, Susan, (2014), *Little Things Long Remembered: Making Your Children Feel Special Every Day,* Iron Gate Press

Dweck, Ph.D., Carol S., (2006), *Mindset: The New Psychology of Success,* Random House

Siegel, Dr. Daniel & **Payne Bryson, Dr. Tina** (2020), *The Power of Showing Up: How Parental Presence Shapes Who Our Kids Become and How Their Brains Get Wired,* Ballantine Books

ABOUT THE AUTHOR

Sybil F. Bull is not just a mother to her seven successful adult children. In addition to being a Mimi, a serial entrepreneur, a faith leader, a coach, a mentor, an international speaker, and a best-selling author, she is also living proof that the essence of parenting lies in embracing the "chaos" with a smile. Her journey challenges the stereotypes of modern motherhood and offers a fresh perspective on raising a family in today's world. Whether you're already a parent, aspiring to become one, or fascinated by the dynamics of a large family, *"Just Appetizers: Building Blocks of Parenting"* is your invitation to explore the depth, complexity, and unparalleled joy of parenting. Join Sybil as she shares her journey, lessons learned, and wisdom garnered from a life filled with love, laughter, and the occasional spot of mayhem.

Sybil and Her 7 Children

9 798999 216400 8